CATCHING A
PLANE

BRENDA CLARKE
ILLUSTRATED BY PETER DENNIS

Kingfisher Books

Advisers: Mary Jane Drummond,
Tutor in Primary Education,
Cambridge Institute of Education, Cambridge
Iris Walkinshaw, Headteacher,
Rushmore Infants School, Hackney, London

Technical advisers: Barry Buttenshaw,
Heathrow Airport Ltd; Jane Johnston and Captain
M. Channing, British Airways.

The author and publisher would also like to thank
Captain P. D. Youngs and Air-stewardess J. Kent
for their help in the preparation of this book.

Kingfisher Books, Grisewood & Dempsey Ltd
Elsley House, 24–30 Great Titchfield Street,
London W1P 7AD

First published in 1988 by Kingfisher Books

BRITISH CATALOGUING IN PUBLICATION DATA
Clarke, Brenda
Catching a plane.—(Stepping stones 4,5,6).
1. Airplanes—Juvenile literature
I. Title   II. Dennis, Peter   III. Series
387.7 HE9776.5
ISBN: 0 86272 338 8

Edited by Vanessa Clarke
Editorial assistant: Camilla Hallinan
Designed by Roger Wade-Walker
Cover designed by Pinpoint Design Company
Phototypeset by Southern Positives and Negatives (SPAN),
Lingfield, Surrey
Colour separations by Newsele Litho Ltd, Milan
Printed in Spain

Contents

DEPARTURES				
Flight	**To**	**Time**	**Remarks**	**Gate**
AF 640	PARIS	09.00	NOW BOARDING	12
PA 432	NEW YORK	09.00	NOW BOARDING	9
LH 049	MUNICH	09.15		6
KF 250	ALICANTE	09.45		15
JL 054	TOKYO	09.50		3
AZ 350	ROME	09.50		10

← Arrivals

KF Airlines

Here we are at the airport. Mum and Dad, my brother Tom and I are off on our holidays. We are going to Spain. It's a long way away so we are catching a plane to fly there.

We have tickets for KF Airlines Flight 250. The flight number is on the indicator board. The board shows all the information about the planes leaving the airport. We have lots of time to find the KF Airlines desk and check in our suitcases.

At the check-in desk the assistant takes our tickets. She uses a computer to find us empty seats on the plane. Then she writes our seat numbers

on four boarding passes – one for each of us. She also weighs our luggage. Each passenger is allowed to take only 20 kilos of baggage, so she makes sure our suitcases are not too heavy.

She sticks KF Airlines labels on each suitcase to show which airport we are flying to in Spain.

The suitcases go along the conveyor belt to the baggage handlers. They read the labels and send the suitcases to the right plane.

Tom can't wait to see the planes. But first
Mum and Dad have to show their passports to
the passport officer. Tom's name and mine are
written inside Mum's passport.

Next we go through the security check. We put
our hand baggage on a conveyor belt. Then we
walk through a metal detector gate.

Mum says that all the passengers have to do this to make sure nobody carries anything dangerous on to the plane.

Our bags roll under an X-ray scanner machine. The security officer sees an X-ray picture on her screen of everything inside the bags. She can even see inside Tom's Ted.

Now we are in the departure lounge waiting for our flight. Out of the window we can see people working on a plane. I think it is our plane because KF Airlines is written on it. Look! Another plane is taking off from the runway.

Water truck

Fuel monitor truck

Underground fuel tank

The engineer fills the fuel tanks in the plane's wings.

That must be our plane.

How do we get on it?

Soon Dad tells us that our plane is ready. It is waiting for us at Gate 15. "Do we get on the plane through a gate?" asks Tom.

10

Runway

Baggage van

K F Airlines

Air jetty

The pilot checks the outside of the plane before take-off.

The tug will push the plane backwards out of its parking space.

Tug

11

At Gate 15 we walk through a tunnel called an air jetty right to the door of the plane. An air-stewardess tells Dad where to find our seats.

We have three seats in one row and one seat in the row in front. On the ceiling there are three lights and a buzzer to call the cabin crew. I can feel cold air blowing in through three funnels.

"Why can't I open the window?" asks Tom. Mum says it is because the plane has to be airtight. The plane flies high in the sky where the air is too thin for us to breathe, so the plane carries its own supply of air.

The pilot and the co-pilot are at the front of
the plane on the flight-deck. The pilot is the
Captain of the plane and always sits in the
left-hand seat. They check all the instruments
to make sure that everything is working
properly. Then the Captain asks the cabin crew
to shut the door of the plane. It is time to go.

Kilo-foxtrot
two-five-zero,
start engines and
proceed to
runway zero-
three.

The stewardess swings the heavy door shut. But, before the plane can leave, the Captain speaks to the air traffic control tower by radio. The air traffic controllers in the tower give instructions to all the planes landing at the airport and taking off. When they give permission, the Captain starts the plane's engines.

Dad is sitting in front of me. I show Tom how
to make a little table with the flap clipped to
the back of Dad's seat. But a stewardess asks
me to put up the flap and fasten my seatbelt.
She shows me the signs: NO SMOKING and
FASTEN SEATBELT. Mum helps Tom with his belt.

FASTEN
SEATBELT

NO SMOKING

The stewardess helps me. Then she stands in
the aisle between the seats and shows us how to
put on a life jacket. The steward asks us to

read the instructions on our safety cards so we will know what to do in an emergency. They both walk down the aisle to make sure that all the passengers have fastened their seatbelts. Then they sit down and fasten their belts too.

The plane is moving slowly along. It feels very bouncy. "We are taxiing to the runway," says Mum. "There are probably planes in front of us, and we must queue up to take off."

Air traffic
control tower

Taxiway

Runway

18

Kilo foxtrot
two-five-zero
changing to
departure
control.

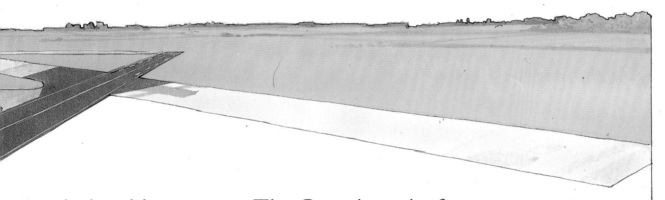

At last it's our turn. The Captain waits for
the take-off signal from the controller.
Then he switches the engines to full power.
The plane rushes faster and faster along the
runway. The engines roar. I feel as if
something is pushing me back into my seat.
Tom holds on tight to Mum's hand.

Now the plane is going fast enough to take
off. Suddenly the nose of the plane lifts.
Whoosh! We're up in the air. We're flying!

"Look at the houses and cars down there," says Tom. Everything on the ground seems to grow smaller and smaller as the plane climbs higher.

Soon there is nothing to see out of the window because we are flying through the clouds. Then suddenly we are above them and the sun is shining brightly.

The pilot speaks over the loudspeaker: "Good morning. This is Captain Wright. We are flying at 500 miles per hour and will soon reach our cruising height of 35,000 feet. Our route today will take us over France. I hope you are enjoying the flight."

Tom wants to know how high 35,000 feet is in metres and Mum and Dad try to work it out. I walk down the aisle to the toilet. Bright lights flicker on automatically when I lock the door.

I'm getting your dinner ready

Have you made it yourself?

I pass the galley on the way back to my seat. The steward inside is taking trays of food out of an oven. I don't feel hungry yet. But the steward says that passengers are always given something to eat on a flight. There are 148 passengers on the plane and their meals are all stored on trays in the plane's tiny galley kitchens.

Back in my seat I pull down the flap in front of me to make a table. The steward and a stewardess roll a trolley along the aisle and give us each a meal tray. Each part of the meal is in its own compartment on the tray. The steward asks if Tom and I would like to meet the Captain and the co-pilot and see the flight-deck after we have eaten.

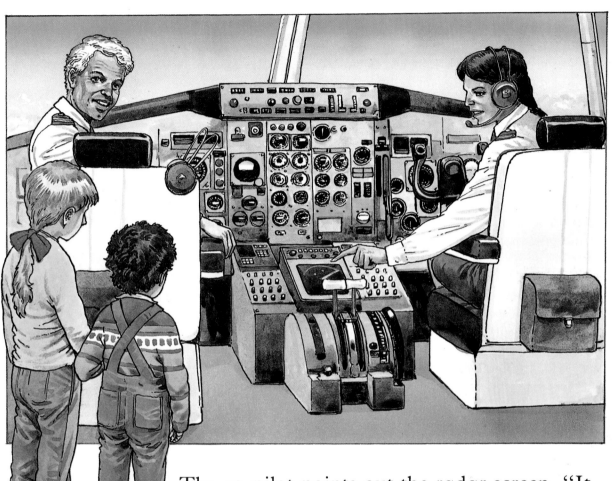

The co-pilot points out the radar screen. "It shows us where the bad weather is," says the Captain. I ask the Captain why he isn't holding the controls. "Don't worry," he says. "The automatic pilot is flying the plane by computer. We can take over at any time and we always use the manual controls when we take off and land."

Mum and Dad change seats when we come back so Mum can read her book. Dad has found a map in the flight magazine. We can see the route our plane is flying and the routes to other cities all over the world.

Then the Captain announces: "We are crossing the Spanish border and shortly we'll begin the descent for landing. Passengers on both sides of the cabin now have an excellent view of the Pyrenees."

Down below, out of the window, the mountain tops are white with snow.

Ding! The FASTEN SEATBELT and NO SMOKING signs come on and we fasten our seatbelts again. Now it is my turn to sit by the window.

The cabin crew check that our seat belts are fastened and that there is no hand baggage blocking the aisle. The Captain and the co-pilot prepare the plane for landing. They lower the plane's wheels and speak to the Spanish air traffic controller by radio.

The plane drops down and down. My ears feel blocked and Dad tells me to swallow to make them feel better. Out of the window, I can see the sea.

On the flight-deck, the Captain waits for the air traffic controller to give permission for our plane to land.

There is another plane in front of ours but soon the runway is clear. The Captain brings the plane down. Everything outside rushes past in a blur. Bump! The wheels touch the ground. The plane is on the runway. The Captain slows the engines which makes them roar loudly. The wheels swish along the ground.

Soon the plane is taxiing slowly towards the terminal building. A marshal waves two bats to guide the Captain to the plane's parking space.

The stewardess tells us to stay in our seats. We have to wait for the engines to stop and for the airport workers to bring steps to the plane's door.

At last we can walk down the passenger steps into the hot sunshine. "Will the Captain go to the beach for a swim?" asks Tom. "No," says Dad. "He probably has to fly the plane back home."

The airport workers are already unloading the baggage. Soon they will get the plane ready for its next flight.

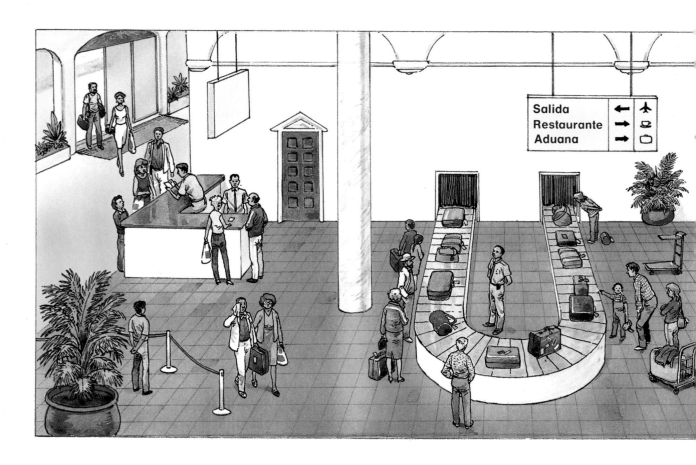

Mum and Dad show their passports to the
Spanish passport officer inside the airport
terminal. Then we wait for our suitcases to
roll in on a conveyor belt. Tom sees one first.
I am looking for the second suitcase.

"Now there's just Customs," says Mum. The
customs officers stop some people and search

their suitcases to make sure they are not carrying things which are not allowed in Spain. They don't want to see inside our suitcases so we can go straight outside.

Another plane is taking off. "Landing was best," says Tom. But I liked taking off and landing and the flight-deck . . . I liked it all.

31

Index